Staring Dementia in the Face

poems by

Lylanne Musselman

Finishing Line Press
Georgetown, Kentucky

Staring Dementia in the Face

Copyright © 2023 by Lylanne Musselman
ISBN 979-8-88838-259-2 First Edition
All rights reserved under International and Pan-American Copyright Conventions.
No part of this book may be reproduced in any manner whatsoever without written permission from the publisher, except in the case of brief quotations embodied in critical articles and reviews.

ACKNOWLEDGMENTS

These poems have appeared or are forthcoming, some in earlier versions, in the following publications:

"Each Day"—*Tipton Poetry Journal,* Issue 40; It was nominated for a Pushcart Prize in 2019, and it is included in the Inverse Poetry Archive, a collection of Hoosier poets, housed at the Indiana State Library.
"Healing Nature"—*Tipton Poetry Journal*, Issue 44
"How to Lose Your Mom Over and Over"—*Silver Birch Press*, 2021
"I Pass Over its Bridges"—*Indianapolis Review*, Winter Issue 2022
"Listening to the Dementia Channel"—*Grand Little Things*, 2021
"Repeat Offender"—*Flying Island*, 2018
"Stolen Memories"—*Last Stanza Poetry Journal*, Issue 6

Publisher: Leah Huete de Maines
Editor: Christen Kincaid
Cover Art: Lylanne Musselman
Author Photo: Sheila Piazza
Cover Design: Elizabeth Maines McCleavy

Order online: www.finishinglinepress.com
also available on amazon.com

Author inquiries and mail orders:
Finishing Line Press
PO Box 1626
Georgetown, Kentucky 40324
USA

Table of Contents

Each Day 1

Healing Nature 2

Lessons Learned 3

Living in Rewind 5

Mind Thief 6

Over the Hill 7

Repeat Offender 9

Another Day Begins 10

Golden Times 12

I Wish… 13

Listening to the Dementia Channel 14

My Poem Wants Me Unstuck 15

A Caretaker's Lament 16

Only Child 18

Bright Blue Message 20

Last Seen at the Nursing Home 21

Visiting Mom 22

Stolen Memories 23

#Your Mom 24

There is a Season 26

How to Lose Your Mom Over and Over 28

I Pass Over its Bridges 29

This May 30

Mourning Again 31

Dedicated to
Keli and Alison, my beloved daughters,
my grandchildren, Codey, Kyli, Scott, Saylor, Damon, and Alex
and my great-grandchildren, Kolby, Colton, and Baker,
all of whom were my support as I moved through the
unchartered waters, living the life of a caregiver

Each Day

She doesn't think she needs anyone
to stay with her, to take care of her—
make sure she eats, make sure she takes meds
at the right time, the right dosage,
make sure she doesn't fall as she toddles
down the hallway like a two-year-old with her walker.
She gets mad when told "you can't stay alone."
Each day, she gets crankier and glares
at me as if I'm her arch enemy.
Me, her only child, who put my freedom
on hold to keep her free from the fate
of the nursing home she dreads. She argues
she's "just fine…" as she repeats herself
every five minutes; as she accuses me
of "stealing" her mail, of being "mean" to her;
as she mockingly calls me "mom" for reminding her
to do mundane things; as she forgets
the birthdays of those she loves, as she
attempts to change TV channels with the mobile phone,
and wonders why it isn't working.

Healing Nature

I hear songbirds chirping and feel calm,
a respite from a world that's filled
with, guns, gaudy lies, and fake news.

A world where my mom talks
to my dead grandma as if she's in
the backseat of my car,

asking what she wants to order
from Dairy Queen. Where mom's falls
become more frequent, where I feel

like her mother telling her to go
to the bathroom, when to go to bed,
that she needs to eat. She fights me

about her bedtime as if she's ten,
I fight with myself as to how much longer
I can deal with being her caregiver,

as she looks at me and asks where I went,
why I won't tell her where her mom is.
The outside world is fighting too

over how much more we can take
without someone to protect us
from the violence, the lies, the poverty.

It's hard not to give up. But the birds
ground me with their frequency—their songs
lift me to Zen, a state where I long to live.

Lessons Learned

As mom falls
into dementia
deeper and faster,
it's hard to watch;
to hear her say
"I can't have
anything wrong…
mom didn't."

She's correct,
grandma didn't
have dementia.
The more I study
the mind's disease,
I see how mom fell
victim—she was
a willing accomplice.

Her mantra,
which she repeats
often, "I don't like to
learn new things"
ties in with new studies:

learning wards off
losing your mind
even if predisposed to it.
She also doesn't
like socializing—
making friends
or visiting people.

I'm relieved
I love to learn,
create new things,
and I cherish
having friends,
so many—who may be
the best medicine
of my life.

Living in Rewind

Mom's demented communication drives me crazy every day, within minutes she repeats herself again and again:
"This is such a pretty day. What is that bird out there?"
"Is there something I can do?" But she continues to sit.

Within minutes she repeats herself again and again:
"What day is this? This slaw is too tough."
"Is there something I can do?" She just continues to sit.
"I wasn't asleep, I was just resting my eyes."

"What day is this? This slaw is too hard to chew."
I know I'm not supposed to get frustrated with her, but I do.
She insists, "I wasn't asleep, I was just resting my eyes."
"It's time to go to bed? But I'm not tired yet."

I know I'm not supposed to get frustrated with her, but I do.
I hear from others, "She's your mom. How lucky are you!"
Every night she says, "It's time to go to bed? I'm not tired yet."
She lashes out at me with such anger and disgust.

I despise hearing, "But she's your mom. You're lucky she's here."
She says, "What a pretty day this is. What is that bird out there?"
She lashes out at me over and over with such anger and disgust.
Mom's repeated dementia sentences drive me crazier every day.

5

Mind Thief

Mom says she doesn't deserve "the goblet" and the linen napkins, amenities she receives during her stay at Morrison Woods, after a fall fractured three ribs. She scoffs at meatloaf and twice-baked potatoes for dinner. She cries because she's so happy I've come to see her, she cries because she doesn't know why she's not getting better, she cries as she flails on the bed while yelling "get me out of this place, take me back to the hospital. I don't like it here!" She asks where dad is—even though she visited him daily these past 10 weeks. She doesn't remember he already had surgery and says, "he's not going to like that!" She sticks her tongue out at me and my daughters. She worries about money, her checkbook, her purse, her wedding ring. Mom misses her two cats. I miss my mom.

Over the Hill
      (Inspired by John Hiatt's Over the Hill)

Who would've guessed
after the hard climb up,
and teetering on over,
that on this side of the hill
I would be taking care of mom
as if she's a young child—
preparing her meals,
prompting potty breaks,
making sure she takes meds
that she keeps hydrated;
taking her to doctor appointments,
and putting her to bed each night.

A lot of others on this side
of the hill are going through this
same drudgery, the same drill, one
we never saw coming as ascending
life's long and steep hill.
Another on this side, a friend,
caring for her young grandson—
full custody, starting over
as if a 20-year-old mother,
she and her husband raising a child,
making his meals, doling out discipline,
taking him to after school activities,
tucking him in bed each night.

Over the hill sure looks different
than what people think:
starting over in our 60s,
doing the type of work
we thought we'd already
paid our dues in—looking forward
to redemption and relaxation.
Instead, we find that it's not
coasting down that hill
into vacations and retirement,
it's scheduling our time
to fit in our own lives
around being another's
full-time caregiver.

Repeat Offender

Nothing prepares you
for the broken record
of your mom's mind
on a circular spin
and with each repeated
phrase you feel yourself
spinning out of control.
You have to remember
she cannot reason
any more than one can
reason with a two-year-old.
Sometimes when you tell
her she can't drive anymore
she argues, cries, and pleads
to give her just one chance.
You tell her you're afraid
for her safety and the safety
of others. She says you can
ride with her and if she does
something bad, you can tell her
to pull over and she will; and
all at once you remember:
a younger, saner mom
who was mad at you
as a young adult,
a passenger in her car.
She floored it on the back roads,
saying she didn't care
if she killed us both. And,
you realize how irrational
she has always been—
when she is not in control.

Another Day Begins

Another morning,
a good mood, ready
to face the day.
I know what I want
to do: write a poem,
make some art, grade
creative writing journals.

First, the cats need fed,
their litter cleaned, then
I put mom's bed rail down,
the guard that allows me
peaceful sleep, after collecting
her clothes, a new Depends,
a washrag, and putting it on her
rollator. Her cue to get up.

I retreat to the kitchen,
crack the eggs, butter toast,
microwave bacon, rinse my
blueberries, a healthy fruit
she's never tried. I dispense
her pills onto her full plate,
and eat my breakfast.

I go check on mom,
who is still in bed. She says,
"did you want me up?"
I say, "that's why your rail
is down." Yet, I know better
than to reason with her.
She says, "I didn't know you
wanted me up. I don't want you
to yell at me." I consider
all the times I haven't yelled—
in the classroom, at my daughters,
at ex-husbands and ex-lovers,
at this day for being another
like every other since being
her caregiver, at her...and
another day begins.

Golden Times

A night out
with old friends
reminiscing
back to a time
when my friends and I
were teens, unburdened
of adult responsibilities,
looking forward
to our futures,

a welcome diversion
from taking care
of my elderly mom
who suffers dementia,
who oftentimes
regresses to living
the distant past
in her mind.

I Wish…

I wish my mom was healthy
and not in dementia decline.
I could be living my own life
without repeating myself
every 10 minutes. I wish
I'd concentrated on writing
earlier in life—would I be
any farther along than I am?
I wish I had the metabolism
from when I was 15, then
I could eat anything I wanted,
drink a lot of sugary Cokes,
never gaining a pound. I wish
someone would come into my life
worthy of my trust and love—
no narcissists or abusers need apply.
I wish life didn't pass by so fast, and
that lessons learned could buy more
time—I'd live into my hundreds.

Listening to the Dementia Channel
    (Or A Day in the Life of Being Mom's Caregiver)

I can't believe the corn has tasseled already, look at it!
What's that bird out there with the red head?
That is what you believe. It's your truth not mine.
What day is this? It doesn't seem like Monday.

What's that bird out there with the red head?
What channel is the Game Show Network?
What day is this? It doesn't seem like Monday.
Your cats won't let me make my bed!

What channel is the Game Show Network?
It's not rained like this all year, has it?
Your cats won't let me make my bed!
I can too drive, give me the keys!

It's not rained like this all year, has it?
This road rides nice for not going anywhere.
I can too drive, give me the keys!
You're not my mom, don't tell me what to do!

This road rides nice for not going anywhere.
Just because you believe it, it doesn't make it true!
You're not my mom, so don't tell me what to do!
The corn has tasseled already, look at it, look at it!

My Poem Wants Me Unstuck

The hardest part about being mom's caregiver
is that it's hard for an independent mind,
one that always seeks freedom over being stuck,
stuck in June and June seems like it's gone on
since January, stuck in Monday and Monday never
changes to Tuesday. Each day is like walking
a treadmill, which I hate because there's never
a change of scenery. My poems like for me to be free,
walk around in nature, see the blooming roses,
hear the cardinal's trill. Instead, I'm bound
every morning fixing breakfast, eggs, bacon, and
getting mom ready for another mundane day.
I do get joy from my bowl of blueberries with whipped
cream. Although my daughter warns they're full of carbs—
I eat them anyway, savoring the color of each one,
tasting the sweetness, as if it's a start of a new poem,
wondering if I washed them well enough to rid them
of pesticides that might deaden my brain cells.

A Caretaker's Lament

You should be glad
"you still have your mom,"
is what people say
who do not know
my situation: frustration.

They don't repeat the identity
of that "pretty bird"
outside on the feeder
fifty times a day, every day.

They don't tell her to drink
her milk, water, any liquid,
constantly because of calls
from her doctors…another UTI.

They don't carry her
heavy, wet Depends
to the outside trash bin
every morning, afternoon, and night—

even though I've reminded her
to go to the bathroom every hour
and she ignores me.

They don't argue with her
as I try to tell her
the next right thing
she needs to do
because she calls me "mom"
(and not in a nice way).

They don't see her primp
with her handheld mirror
like she's some 13-year-old
wishing for a boyfriend.

They don't see her kiss
some old boyfriend, 10 years her junior
with such passion it makes me gag—

knowing my dad
has been dead less than
five months and I never saw
her kiss him like that.

They don't know
she never mentions my dad,
unless she's accusing me
of acting "just like him."

They don't clean her shit
up off the bathroom floor
or argue with her about pulling
her Depends down too soon.

They don't have to watch
the Game Show Network,
day in and day out…
a constant—Family Feud.

Only Child

As an only child I wanted a sibling,
one who would play Mousetrap
with me since mom wouldn't,
I could play it at my cousin's house,
and loved the thrill of escaping the trap
of being home, alone, without anyone
to play with. My brother could play
badminton on the other side of the net,
my sister could be in competition
not to be left holding the Old Maid.

In my teens, I joked about wanting a sibling—
a boy close to my age—
a brother to protect me from unwanted cat calls,
who'd shoot baskets with his tomboy sister.
A sister who'd make me an aunt
that I'd never become.

In early adult years my wishes for a sibling
got sidetracked as I got caught up looking
for love and walking down the aisle
into three failed marriages, into the money woes
of being a single mom, and finding myself,
in and out of more romances, being
a non-traditional student. A lover.
Cobbling together an adjunct career.
I had no time to entertain a brother or a sister.

In later years, an empty nester I pride
myself in the sisterly love of my two daughters,
I made sure they did not live my lonely child fate.
Still, I yearn for my sibling I never got. Someone
who helps share the load of aging parents—
dad's untimely death, mom's dementia.

A brother to share childhood memories—
who laughs when we recall dad mooing
at the cows as we'd drive past. A sister
who cringes at the looks mom gave us
when she thought we were laughing at her
behind her back. A sibling to remember
searching for the prize in Cracker Jack, or
cracking up at The Monkees on Monday night
while mom and dad sat in silence.

Bright Blue Message

I first heard the chirps
as I walked an early morning
sunlit path. In the bushes
a glint of blue. Flitting
from branch to branch
an Indigo Bunting. He was
singing love songs. Free
from gloomy worries. He
thrilled me with hope
for a fleeting moment.

For this moment I didn't fret
about the way my world
feels like it's spinning
out of control—the novel
coronavirus spreading
closer, how long before
it touches a loved one or
visits mom's nursing home,
where I turned over
her care due to dementia.

Not thinking of how
poorly the president
has handled this pandemic.
Of how his lies are killing
unsuspecting people—
unprepared as sitting ducks
at an outdoor shooting range.

I didn't think about paths
not taken. The what ifs.
Life is beautiful if I live
in the moment: I receive
unexpected visitations like the
spirited Indigo Bunting
who lifted me to a higher plane.

Last Seen at the Nursing Home

Mom sees the dead. She's not a psychic.
She doesn't believe in spirits, instead
her mom, dad, aunts, uncles, ex-lovers
and my dad are alive, inside her head.
When I visit her I pretend the stories
she tells are true. I can't show her how
startled I am when she says Uncle Dudley
visited yesterday, or when she's mad
because dad has not. She cries
when she sees me, she cries when I leave.

When I ask her why she's crying, she says
she's so happy to see me. I see her shrink
inside clothes that swallow her once statuesque
body. She says she can't believe I "finally came
to rescue her," to get her out of "this awful place"
and into her world, where she believes
she still works at my uncle's restaurant.

A world where she feels she can walk out
on her own two feet, where she won't fall
flat on her face, crack a few bones,
one where she can drive her wheelchair
down the road as if it's her cardinal red convertible,
pull into some driveway, declaring she's home.
A world where I'd never worry that I'd see her picture
come across my phone announcing her silver alert
or worse.

Visiting Mom

I feel like I fall down the groundhog hole
every time I visit mom who suffers dementia,
who lives anywhere in her mind but now.
It's confusing and unsettling hearing her talk
about my grandparents as if they're living
down the street. She waits for them to come
visit her, and tells me I need to tell them
to clean out her room upstairs because she's
coming home. One day she tells me her life
was wonderful with dad, he was hers until
I came along. The child she took great effort
in her good old days to divide my love for dad
and give it all to her, since she felt he didn't
treat her the way she wanted. I try to live
in the present, but get yanked back into the past,
where mom kept me off balance, in doubt
of what really happened in our household. Now,
with her dementia it's hard to tell the difference.

Stolen Memories

I

A 12-point buck has become a trophy
for some middle-aged guy who needs
to mount bragging rights to camouflage
his mundane life: gulping beer to numb
feelings, to forget failed dreams and
small paychecks—no consideration
for this buck's life snuffed out in an instant,
from does waiting for him with nesting fawns,
from memories of running
through the woods, of another rut season,
of finding fresh berries, crunchy
acorns, and tender leafy greens.

II

Mom closes her eyes to the world
knowing her best days are behind her:
standing tall in mini-skirts and go-go boots,
of meeting Tom Jones, slinging panties
on stage, she's missing moments
laughing with great grandchildren, holding
her newest great-great, forgetting loved ones
by the day and her mind can't tell her why.
She can't know the freedom of running,
now confined to a wheelchair. She feels
a burden to her family, and heaven knows
she should've eaten more tomatoes, walnuts,
blueberries, and fresh leafy greens.

#Your Mom

Mom in dementia lockdown
in the locked down nursing home
#has not kept her from keeping
my phone blown up as nurses
call to report #your mom
has fallen out of her wheelchair
again #another call #your mom
has taken up with a man and you
should know #her hand is on his
leg #the nurse laughs but says
#your mom has got a smile on
her face #days later another nurse
reports #your mom got her nails done
and that man picked out her nail
color #pink #I know mom's color
has always been fire engine red
#your mom and that man played
some slapping game with their hands
#your mom has a big bruise on the back
of her hand #thought you should know
#days later a nurse calls #your mom needs
moved out of lockdown since she's not
a flight risk in her wheelchair #we caught
that man trying to put #your mom into bed
and we cannot have them falling #breaking bones
and the nurse says #your mom is a man magnet
#we laugh #I know dementia has not diminished
her #flirting trait #today the nursing home
called again #your mom fell asleep in her
wheelchair #she fell out of it onto the floor
and has a laceration on her forehead but
no broken bones #I wish she had a Prince
Charming to #catch her frail body

There is a Season...

I look out the window, bright
yellow leaves fall to the ground.
The nursing home calls, mom's fever
has spiked. I can't visit because of
the pandemic. When I call, she cries or
talks about her world—
one where her parents are alive,
one where she thinks
neighbors are selling drugs,
one where she's driving to Eaton,
if she can only find her keys.

Every winter I'm reminded
of both grandmas passing—
two days before Christmas
a heavy lesson at 12:
loved ones don't stay
with us forever, at 43
my other cherished grandma's
expected hospital release
on Saturday, that cold Friday
my visit after *Good Will Hunting*,
the sterile white flat sheets on her
vacant bed shocks me. The emptiness
chills me still.

That spring I never wanted
to take grandpa to the nursing home.
In my mid-20s, it was hard to accept
his stroke that left him the shell
of the "Bobo" I loved. Mom and uncle
wouldn't... "Work" they said.
Grandma couldn't drive.
I remember the whiff of lilacs
as my cousin and I took him inside.

The cries and loud hollering of residents
alarmed me. His cries and begging us
not to leave him there still haunt me.

Summer bloomed around our house,
Heirloom Roses, climbing Clematis,
dad had a green thumb,
but he never liked June—
the month his father died,
a broken man—
on those Sharpsville railroad tracks,
leaving behind eleven children,
one on the way. His father promised dad
new shoes that day. At 13 years old,
he discovered life wasn't fair.
The June dad died, I discovered
crammed in his closet:
old shoes, news shoes, some never worn.

I look out the window, bright yellow
leaves fall to the ground.
My mind drifts to a time
when I was a child, asking my parents
if they were going to die.
"Not for a long time, honey,"
mom said with a smile. Dad was silent
as usual. I worry—
orphaned and alone.

How to Lose Your Mom Over and Over

After her hard falls, more messy accidents,
you give in to the reality mom is too hard to handle
at home, since dementia has deteriorated her health
in these two years you've been sole caregiver.

Confined to her wheelchair, it's a mystery how
she escaped the first nursing home you thought
extremely secure. You're thankful she didn't become
a statewide Silver Alert in that chilly October air.

With mom settled into a new facility, you make it through
a first Christmas without her at family gatherings. Visit her
four or five times a week. Adapt to other's well-meaning phrase:
"You're so lucky! At least you still have your mom."

Never expect a pandemic lockdown of nursing homes,
or that her hugs from last March will have to hold you.
Call her often, she doesn't understand why you're not visiting,
she cries hearing your voice, you never know how to hang up.

Summer, a reprieve of outdoor visits, with masks, six feet apart,
no hugs, no touching. Hard for her to understand the need
for distance, she accuses you of not caring whether she's dead
or alive, then begs to drive. So much for happy visits.

In autumn, her nursing home locks down again. You're thankful
they have no Covid-19 cases. Until they do in late October,
then the call: "Your mom has a fever spike." Nurses assure you
she's tested negative twice. In November, she's isolated

in the Covid unit, afraid and alone. Her nurse calls several times:
"Your mom is yelling nonstop! We don't know how to calm her down."
Upsetting since no visits are allowed. That Monday, go stand outside
her window. She recognizes you, but she's a shell of herself.

Her death glares you in the face. Hospice needs to be called.
On Friday the 13th: "Honey, your mom is going to meet Jesus.
It won't be long." These words are hard to hear anytime,
but when you can't be there, it's cruel. You're isolated, lost.

You hope she's in a better place. Know she hated the rest "home,"
being forced to play Bingo, being limited to that wheelchair,
never knowing why her parents weren't visiting.

I Pass Over its Bridges

I cross the Mississinewa River
to get groceries, to meet friends,
to go to church, to carry art to exhibits,
to visit the cemetery where my ancestors are buried.
Each time I pass over its bridges, singing
"Can't Buy Me Love" at the top of my lungs
while riding in the backseat of my grandparent's car
on our trips for ice cream at Dairy Dream,
of Mom before dementia set in, always driving,
of Dad laughing when we'd cross
the wooden bridge in Granville,
its rickety racket making me panic,
of my own daughters giggling over boys
in the backseat as we drove home
from miniature golf or from Pizza King,
of Mark singing "Sun Arise" along with Alice Cooper
in his red Vega after one of our movie dates,
of riding school bus number 26 to Delta on Highway 3,
of Bill and I sailing south, heading toward our honeymoon
in Florida, of crossing it pregnant, traveling home
with two daughters three years apart,
of driving to work in Muncie
selling sweepers as a single mom,
after carrying years of marital
fear, unkind words, and tears
across that bridge, of seeing
that bald eagle perched
among autumn leaves,
after leaving mom in hospice,
of driving home, alone,
across the familiar river.

This May

It has been a hard month: a Mother's Day without
a mother, her first birthday not on earth, another ending
of a semester, the pressure of overcommitting as if
me, myself, and I were three persons up to multiple tasks,
which did get done, but as I grow older my bones
get more weary. And, for every bit of good news—a normal
mammogram, there's a hit—I have osteoporosis.

My doctor warns me not to fall, as if this is not a normal goal
I've had since a child. Who does like to fall? Some daredevil
I suppose. She tells me when I turn 65 later this year and
Medicare kicks in, bone meds should top my wish list.
At my age, I don't take meds, a medical oddity to most but one
I'm proud of and intend to keep—so I opt for taking a high dose
of Calcium with daily vitamins—even though it won't grow bone.

Weight bearing exercises are part of my new regime. Walk more—
I've been intending to after the weather gets nicer, after Covid
restrictions are lifted, after grading is done, after my next painting,
after more poems are written - it all weighs me down on the couch,
but creativity lifts my spirits—as I tend to my brittle bones that carry
my heavy thoughts and thighs through this harsh world.

Mourning Again

When looking at Facebook,
you never know what you might see.
It may be an old friend, you haven't seen
in years, or a funny meme. Maybe
a political post that makes you cringe or
contemplate if you ever knew that
person or why they're on your timeline,
but sometimes a post causes an unexpected
emotional upheaval, like the one when I scrolled
onto a post of a former student. It was
simple enough, a beautiful picture
of her elderly mom in a nursing home bed,
her big brown eyes wide, mouth agape—
her pure joy shining through. The student
wrote: *The look on my mother's face after
not seeing me in over a year.* Her post
penetrated me in a way I didn't expect.
Through tears, it was hard to comment:
I'm so happy for you both. Even though
I did and I truly was. I was sad from being robbed
by the pandemic of my chance to see
that sparkle in mom's eyes, her smile
when finally seeing me again
if I'd gotten to visit her in the nursing home
one more time.

Lylanne Musselman is an award-winning poet, playwright, and visual artist. Her work has appeared in *Pank, The New Verse News, Rose Quartz Magazine, Last Stanza Poetry Journal* and *The Ekphrastic Review,* among others. Recently, one of her poems was selected as the featured poem in *Tipton Poetry Journal,* Issue # 48 Spring 2021. Musselman's work has appeared in many anthologies, including *The Indianapolis Anthology* (Belt Publishing, 2021). She is the author of six chapbooks, including *Weathering Under the Cat* (Finishing Line Press, 2017), and *Paparazzi for the Birds* (Red Mare 16, 2018), and is also the author of the full-length poetry collection, *It's Not Love, Unfortunately* (Chatter House Press, 2018). Musselman is a three-time Pushcart Prize nominee, and her poems are included in the Inverse Poetry Archive, a collection of Hoosier poets, housed at the Indiana State Library. She is the Director of Blackford County Arts Center of Arts Place.

www.ingramcontent.com/pod-product-compliance
Lightning Source LLC
Chambersburg PA
CBHW022125090426
42743CB00008B/1007